Preventing Catastrophic Nuclear Terrorism

DATE DUE	
DEC 0 1 2006	
MAY 2 2 2007	
MAY 2 2 2007	

BRODART, CO.   Cat. No. 23-221-003

Charles D. Ferguson

CSR NO. 11, MARCH 2006
COUNCIL ON FOREIGN RELATIONS

9980985
m

Founded in 1921, the Council on Foreign Relations is an independent, national membership organization and a nonpartisan center for scholars dedicated to producing and disseminating ideas so that individual and corporate members, as well as policymakers, journalists, students, and interested citizens in the United States and other countries, can better understand the world and the foreign policy choices facing the United States and other governments. The Council does this by convening meetings; conducting a wide-ranging Studies program; publishing *Foreign Affairs*, the preeminent journal covering international affairs and U.S. foreign policy; maintaining a diverse membership; sponsoring Independent Task Forces and Special Reports; and providing up-to-date information about the world and U.S. foreign policy on the Council's website, www.cfr.org.

THE COUNCIL TAKES NO INSTITUTIONAL POSITION ON POLICY ISSUES AND HAS NO AFFILIATION WITH THE U.S. GOVERNMENT. ALL STATEMENTS OF FACT AND EXPRESSIONS OF OPINION CONTAINED IN ITS PUBLICATIONS ARE THE SOLE RESPONSIBILITY OF THE AUTHOR OR AUTHORS.

Council Special Reports (CSRs) are concise policy briefs, produced to provide a rapid response to a developing crisis or contribute to the public's understanding of current policy dilemmas. CSRs are written by individual authors—who may be Council fellows or acknowledged experts from outside the institution—in consultation with an advisory committee, and typically take sixty days or less from inception to publication. The committee serves as a sounding board and provides feedback on a draft report. It usually meets twice—once before a draft is written and once again when there is a draft for review; however, advisory committee members, unlike Task Force members, are not asked to sign off on the report or to otherwise endorse it. Once published, CSRs are posted on the Council's website.

For further information about the Council or this Special Report, please write to the Council on Foreign Relations, 58 East 68th Street, New York, NY 10021, or call the Communications office at 212-434-9400. Visit our website at www.cfr.org.

CONTENTS

Foreword   v

Acknowledgments   vii

Council Special Report   1

    The Threat   1

    Gaps in the International Response   9

    Recommendations   25

About the Author   33

FOREWORD

A nuclear attack by terrorists against the United States has the potential to make the terrorist attacks of September 11, 2001, look like a historical footnote. In addition to the immediate horrific devastation, such an attack could cost trillions of dollars in damages, potentially sparking a global economic depression. Although, during the 2004 presidential campaign, President George W. Bush and Democratic challenger Senator John F. Kerry agreed that terrorists armed with nuclear weapons worried them more than any other national security threat, the U.S. government has yet to elevate nuclear terrorism prevention to the highest priority. Despite several U.S. and international programs to secure nuclear weapons and the materials to make them, major gaps in policy remain.

This report makes clear what is needed to reduce the possibility of nuclear terrorism. It identifies where efforts have fallen short in securing and eliminating nuclear weapons and weapons-usable nuclear materials, and it offers realistic recommendations to plug these gaps in the U.S. and international response. The result is a clear primer on a critical subject and a set of practical proposals that policymakers would be wise to consider carefully.

Richard N. Haass
President
Council on Foreign Relations
March 2006

ACKNOWLEDGMENTS

During the course of writing this report, I consulted with an advisory group that met twice to discuss how to prevent catastrophic nuclear terrorism. At these meetings and at subsequent one-on-one discussions, the advisers provided insightful comments. I am grateful to Lee Feinstein for chairing the advisory meetings and for providing excellent feedback on an early draft. I thank the following people who contributed their expertise, either as members of the group or separately: John P. Barker, Matthew Bunn, Deepti Choubey, Harold A. Feiveson, Lisa E. Gordon-Hagerty, William Happer, Lukas H. Haynes, Siegfried S. Hecker, Laura S. H. Holgate, Benjamin Huberman, Fred C. Iklé, Spurgeon M. Keeny Jr., Alan Kuperman, Paul Leventhal, Michael A. Levi, Edwin Lyman, Michael M. May, Richard A. Meserve, Marvin Miller, William C. Potter, Joan B. Rohlfing, Ivan Safranchuk, Leonard S. Spector, Francis Slakey, Henry D. Sokolski, Armando Travelli, Frank N. von Hippel, Fred Wehling, and Peter D. Zimmerman, as well as several U.S. government officials, who wish to remain anonymous. I also appreciate the helpful comments from a Miami-based group of Council members on an early draft.

Senior officers and staff of the Council provided essential advice and support. I am grateful for the encouragement of President Richard N. Haass. James Lindsay, the director of Studies, gave excellent advice during the drafting process for restructuring the report. In addition, I greatly appreciate the work done by research associates Divya Reddy and Todd Robinson. Thanks are also well deserved for the Council's publishing team of Patricia Dorff and Molly Graham and for the communications team of Lisa Shields and Anya Schmemann.

This publication was made possible, in part, by a grant from the Carnegie Corporation of New York. I also greatly appreciate the support provided by the John D. and Catherine T. MacArthur Foundation for the Council's science and technology program. The statements made and views expressed in this report are solely my responsibility. I am indebted to Catharine Ferguson for her unwavering support.

Charles D. Ferguson

THE THREAT

The threat of a nuclear attack by terrorists has never been greater. Over the past two decades, terrorist violence and destructiveness have grown. As the September 11, 2001, attacks demonstrated, al-Qaeda and al-Qaeda–inspired terrorists desire to inflict mass casualties. Al-Qaeda and other terrorist organizations have expressed interest in and searched for unconventional means of attack, such as chemical, biological, radiological, and nuclear weapons. Of these weapons, only a nuclear detonation will guarantee immediate massive destruction.

A nuclear explosion would immediately devastate the heart of a city and could kill hundreds of thousands of people. In the longer term, hundreds of thousands more could suffer from radiation sickness and cancer, and thousands of square miles of property would experience radioactive contamination requiring several years and billions of dollars to decontaminate. The broader economic costs of the attack could soar into the trillions of dollars, potentially threatening the national economy and even disrupting the global economy.

The probability of nuclear attack has increased because traditional deterrence—threatening assured destruction against a valued asset such as a national territory—does not work against the terrorist groups most likely to covet nuclear weapons. Such groups are usually not tied to a particular geographic location. Moreover, these terrorist organizations are often guided by religious, quasi-religious, or cult leaders who align themselves with a supreme being rather than with a nation-state that needs protection.

TERRORIST PATHWAYS TO A NUCLEAR BOMB

To launch a nuclear attack, terrorists must first obtain a nuclear bomb. They could do this in three ways: by stealing it, buying it, or building it. All three pathways pose significant constraints to terrorists, but one cannot discount any of these possible routes to catastrophic nuclear terrorism.

With about twenty-seven thousand nuclear weapons in the arsenals of eight nations (Britain, China, France, India, Israel, Pakistan, Russia, and the United States), terrorists appear to have a target-rich environment.[1] All but about one thousand of these weapons reside in two countries: Russia and the United States.[2]

The theft of a nuclear weapon is a staple of movies such as *The Peacemaker* and television shows such as *24*. In practice, such thefts are difficult to carry out. Often considered the "crown jewels" of a nuclear-armed nation's security, nuclear weapons are usually rigorously guarded. But being difficult to steal does not mean impossible. In particular, transporting and deploying nuclear weapons outside of highly secure, central storage sites can increase susceptibility to theft. In December 2004, the U.S. National Intelligence Council warned, "Russian authorities twice thwarted terrorist efforts to reconnoiter nuclear weapon storage sites in 2002" and that terrorists inside Russia also "showed a suspicious amount of interest in the transportation of nuclear munitions."[3]

Even if a nuclear weapon is stolen, terrorists must find a way to activate it. Security and arming devices on most nuclear weapons may block terrorists from using these weapons. For example, specialized security codes called permissive action links (PALs) are required to unlock U.S. nuclear weapons. These electronic locks allow only a limited number of tries to enter the correct code before the weapon disables itself. The more advanced nuclear weapon states of Britain, China, France, and Russia reportedly use similar security systems. Although most Russian nuclear weapons are believed to be equipped with PALs, an unknown number of older Russian tactical nuclear arms may not have this security system. Most of these weapons may have been dismantled or are scheduled for dismantlement, but some may still be deployed. It is unknown whether

---

[1] North Korea also may have a small nuclear arsenal containing, at most, eight weapons. Although the North Korean government said, in February 2005, that it has nuclear arms, it has not unambiguously demonstrated this capability.

[2] For the most up-to-date estimates of the world's nuclear arsenals, see the latest issues of the Natural Resources Defense Council's "Nuclear Notebook" in the *Bulletin of the Atomic Scientists*, available at www.thebulletin.org.

[3] National Intelligence Council, *Annual Report to Congress on the Safety and Security of Russian Nuclear Facilities and Military Forces*, December 2004, available at http://www.cia.gov/nic/special_ russiannuke04 .html.

India, Israel, and Pakistan use PALs, although the United States in recent years may have provided PAL assistance to Pakistan.

Safeing, arming, firing, and fusing (SAFF) procedures also can enhance the security of nuclear weapons. To make a SAFF-equipped weapon ready for detonation, it has to undergo a specific sequence of changes in altitude, acceleration, or other parameters. Even if a terrorist group seized an intact nuclear weapon, the terrorists may not be able to use it unless they had access to codes and information about SAFF procedures.

Although one cannot rule out widespread collusion among insiders to provide information about SAFF procedures or PAL codes, the barriers against successful terrorist acquisition and detonation of nuclear weapons securely guarded in arsenals appear extremely difficult to surmount. Nonetheless, serious concerns remain about the security of Pakistani nuclear weapons and Russian tactical nuclear weapons, especially those that are relatively portable, that may not possess integral security mechanisms such as PALs, or that are not in secure central storage. In sum, stealing a nuclear weapon appears to be a very unlikely pathway for terrorists to detonate a nuclear explosive.

Buying a Nuclear Weapon

Terrorists might buy (or be given) a nuclear weapon by a nuclear state. However, both established nuclear powers and nuclear-armed "rogue" states such as North Korea are unlikely to cooperate. Leaders of these countries know that if they are caught transferring nuclear weapons to terrorists, their states would likely suffer devastating retaliation. Despite the harsh rhetoric of current Iranian political leaders, similar calculations would likely influence Iran, which is believed to be five to ten years away from acquiring the capability to make nuclear weapons.

Of course, deterrence hinges on making a credible retaliatory threat and having credible evidence that the transfer of a nuclear weapon has occurred. Concerning the credible threat, the United States clearly warned in the 2002 "National Strategy to Combat Weapons of Mass Destruction" that "it reserves the right to respond with overwhelming force—including through resort to all of our options—to the use of weapons of mass destruction (WMD) against the United States, our forces abroad, and friends and allies."[4]

Gathering credible "smoking gun" evidence, however, confronts substantial technical challenges. A nuclear explosion produces a complex mix of radioactive debris, which depends sensitively on the weapon's design. In recent years, the United States has undertaken a research program to analyze such evidence to identify a detonated weapon's origin. According to the U.S. Defense Threat Reduction Agency, the nuclear forensics and domestic nuclear event attribution program became operational last year and has made significant progress, but the United States continues to improve this program.[5] Although the exact budget for this program is hard to cull from the U.S. government's open budget, officials familiar with the program acknowledge that it is funded at relatively modest levels of a few tens of millions of dollars annually.

More likely routes for terrorists to buy or be given a nuclear weapon involve corruption among nuclear custodians, black markets, or a coup that brings to power officials sympathetic to terrorist causes. In these respects, Pakistan stands out as a vexing security concern. First, it has a relatively new nuclear command and control system. Second, al-Qaeda and Taliban forces have established a formidable presence in the region. Third, some elements of Pakistan's Inter-Services Intelligence (ISI) agency sympathize with the Taliban, although the extent to which the ISI has access to Pakistan's nuclear arsenal is unclear. Fourth, Pakistani President Pervez Musharraf has twice been the target of assassination attempts. Fifth, the most infamous nuclear black market originated in Pakistan. Dr. Abdul Qadeer Khan, a Pakistani metallurgist and the so-called father of Pakistan's nuclear weapons program, ran a nuclear distribution network that sprawled across Europe, Africa, and Asia and supplied nuclear programs in Iran, Libya, and North Korea. Although no evidence has emerged that Khan's network sold nuclear materials or weapons to terrorists, his network did sell blueprints for a nuclear bomb to Libya. Conceivably, terrorists or criminals may have obtained or eventually could obtain this information. The Khan network also demonstrates that the Pakistani nuclear establishment is vulnerable to an insider threat.

---

[4] White House, *National Strategy to Combat Weapons of Mass Destruction*, Washington, DC, December 2002, p. 3.
[5] William J. Broad, "New Team Plans to Identify Nuclear Attackers," *New York Times*, February 2, 2006.

No terrorist organization currently has the ability to produce weapons-usable nuclear materials. Therefore, to build nuclear weapons, terrorists would have to acquire already made highly enriched uranium (HEU) or plutonium. HEU does not exist in nature, and plutonium occurs naturally in only trace amounts.

Naturally occurring samples of uranium only contain a very small fraction (0.7 percent) of the type of uranium that readily fissions and releases the energy that can fuel nuclear reactors or nuclear weapons. This type is the isotope uranium-235. (Isotopes of the same chemical element have virtually identical chemical properties but distinctly different nuclear properties.) To make a sample of uranium useful for fueling most commercial nuclear power plants, the concentration of uranium-235 is increased, or enriched, so that the amount of uranium-235 in the enriched product is 3 to 5 percent of the total amount. This product is called low enriched uranium (LEU). The concentration of uranium-235 in LEU is too low to power a nuclear weapon. Further enrichment is required to produce weapons-usable uranium.

By definition, highly enriched uranium consists of 20 percent or more of uranium-235. Although HEU of any enrichment level, in principle, can power a nuclear weapon, the greater the enrichment level, the less HEU is needed to make a weapon because of the higher concentration of the fissile isotope uranium-235. Typically, nuclear weapons use uranium that is enriched to 90 percent or more in uranium-235. This material is termed weapons-grade uranium. Nonetheless, even 80 percent enriched uranium can fuel nuclear weapons, as was the case with the Hiroshima bomb.

The only significant technical hurdle to making the Hiroshima bomb was the industrial-scale effort needed to enrich the uranium. At least one terrorist group is known to have tried to enrich uranium. It failed, largely because enrichment is an extremely challenging process, requiring the resources only available to large commercial enterprises or to nation-states.[6] Even some countries have failed to master uranium enrichment. For example, despite making a concerted effort in the 1980s, Saddam Hussein's Iraq was unable to enrich enough uranium for a nuclear bomb. Iran has also

---

[6] In 1993, Aum Shinrikyo tried to mine uranium in Australia. Some of Aum's scientists investigated the possibility of enriching uranium, but the technical challenges proved insurmountable.

struggled with achieving this technological development. Lacking access to uranium enrichment facilities, terrorists would need to seize existing caches of HEU.

Unfortunately, HEU stockpiles are plentiful, with about 1,850 metric tons available globally—enough fissile material to make tens of thousands of nuclear bombs.[7] The vast majority of HEU stockpiles are under military control. Russia and the United States possess an estimated 1,720 metric tons of HEU for weapons purposes and naval propulsion. Britain, China, and France hold tens of metric tons of HEU. Pakistan and South Africa have HEU stockpiles that run upward of several hundred kilograms, enough to make dozens of crude nuclear weapons. Smaller amounts of HEU are contained in more than forty countries with civilian nuclear programs. Still, many of the more than 120 research reactors and related facilities within these countries have enough HEU in each location to make a nuclear bomb.[8] The HEU stockpiles most vulnerable to theft are those located in Pakistan, Russia, and many of the countries with civilian reactor facilities.

Like enriching uranium, making plutonium is currently beyond the capability of terrorists without state-sponsorship. Nuclear reactors to produce plutonium and reprocessing plants to extract plutonium from spent reactor fuel require the type of financial and industrial resources only available to states. Therefore, in order to produce a nuclear weapon, terrorists would need to seize plutonium from existing stockpiles or receive aid from a state.

As with HEU, plutonium exists in both military and civilian sectors. Global military stockpiles contain more than 250 metric tons of plutonium—enough to make tens of thousands of nuclear bombs. The United States and Russia possess more than 90 percent of this material, whereas Britain, China, France, India, Israel, North Korea, and Pakistan own the remainder. The United States and Russia have declared approximately one hundred metric tons of plutonium as excess to defense needs, but they have yet to render this material into non-weapons-usable form. In addition, Britain has declared some 4.4 tons as excess to its defense needs. The United States, Russia, Britain, and France

---

[7] David Albright and Kimberly Kramer, "Fissile Material: Stockpiles Still Growing," *Bulletin of the Atomic Scientists*, November/December 2004, pp. 14–16. This most up-to-date estimate is relevant for stockpiles accumulated as of the end of 2003.
[8] U.S. General Accounting Office, *DOE Needs to Take Action to Further Reduce the Use of Weapons-usable Uranium in Civilian Research Reactors*, GAO-04-807, July 2004, p. 28.

have stopped producing plutonium for weapons purposes. China may also have stopped military plutonium production, but it has never made an official announcement. Barring pressure to halt production, India, Israel, North Korea, and Pakistan will likely continue creating plutonium for their weapons programs.

Civilian plutonium stockpiles also pose a risk for use in nuclear weapons. Although some experts continue to doubt the feasibility of employing reactor-grade plutonium in nuclear bombs, scientific authorities such as the U.S. Department of Energy and the U.S. National Academy of Sciences have stated that this material is weapons-usable.[9] More than a dozen countries hold more than 230 metric tons of plutonium that have been separated from spent nuclear fuel. In this separated form, plutonium is less secure than plutonium embedded in spent fuel. Because spent nuclear fuel tends to be highly radioactive, it provides a protective barrier to acquisition by terrorists or criminals who do not have access to special handling gear. Globally, more than thirteen hundred metric tons of plutonium are contained in spent nuclear fuel. The rate of reprocessing this spent fuel to separate plutonium exceeds the rate of consumption of the plutonium as reactor fuel. Based on the latest unofficial estimate, the global stockpile of civilian plutonium in separated form is growing at the rate of ten metric tons per year.[10] This translates into hundreds of terrorist- or state-constructed nuclear bombs per year.

Should terrorists obtain HEU or plutonium, they then confront the hurdle of constructing a bomb. The Manhattan Project designed and built the two basic types of nuclear bombs: a gun-type device and an implosion-type device. Most of the intellectual effort went into developing the implosion-type bomb, which is much more technically challenging than a gun-type bomb. The gun-type bomb simply shoots one lump of highly enriched uranium into another to start an explosive chain reaction. This type of nuclear weapon can only use HEU to produce a high-yield explosion. Because the Manhattan Project scientists were so confident that this bomb would work, they did not conduct a full-scale nuclear test. The gun-type bomb was first used against Hiroshima.

---

[9] U.S. National Academy of Sciences, *Management and Disposition of Excess Weapons Plutonium* (Washington, DC: National Academy Press, 1994), pp. 32–33; and U.S. Department of Energy, Office of Arms Control and Nonproliferation, *Final Nonproliferation and Arms Control Assessment of Weapons-Usable Fissile Material Storage and Excess Plutonium Disposition Alternatives* (Washington, DC: Department of Energy, NN-0007, 1997).

[10] Institute for Science and International Security, *Global Stocks of Nuclear Explosive Materials, End 2003*, September 2005, available at http://www.isis-online.org/global_stocks/end2003/tableofcontents.html.

Although a gun-type bomb is relatively easy to construct, it requires fairly large amounts of HEU to explode. Terrorists would need about fifty kilograms (110 pounds) of weapons-grade HEU to make a Hiroshima-yield bomb. By using special techniques, terrorists could try to reduce the fissile material requirements. Still, acquiring enough HEU remains the most significant barrier to building a gun-type device.

In contrast to a gun-type bomb, an implosion-type bomb can use either plutonium or HEU. This bomb rapidly implodes, or squeezes, the fissile material into a chain-reacting mass that then explodes. Fortunately, substantial technical barriers hamper terrorist efforts to build an implosion device. For instance, machining and assembling the parts for an implosion device are more difficult than making and fitting together the components of a gun device. Moreover, triggering the implosion demands greater technical skills and specialized equipment than activating the assembly of a gun-type bomb. However, an implosion-type bomb offers the advantage of requiring about half the HEU, approximately twenty-five kilograms (fifty-five pounds) of weapons-grade uranium, than that needed for a gun-type bomb. Also, compared to HEU, less plutonium, about four to ten kilograms (nine to twenty-two pounds), is needed to make an implosion bomb.

Terrorists would be aided by the fact that they would not need to build weapons that would meet military requirements. Professional militaries demand well-tested weapons with reliable explosive yields. Terrorists, in contrast, need a weapon that will produce any appreciable damaging yield. A crude HEU gun-type bomb has a high probability of producing a massively destructive explosion.[11] Moreover, skilled terrorists could make this type of weapon without state assistance.[12] The truly onerous barrier for nuclear terrorists is acquiring enough HEU.

---

[11] Luis W. Alvarez, *Adventures of a Physicist* (New York: Basic Books, 1988); Richard L. Garwin and Georges Charpak, *Megawatts and Megatons: The Future of Nuclear Power and Nuclear Weapons* (Chicago: University of Chicago Press, 2002), p. 313; and Union of Concerned Scientists, *Scientists' Letter on Exporting Nuclear Material*, September 2003.

[12] J. Carson Mark, Theodore Taylor, Eugene Eyster, William Maraman, and Jacob Wechsler, "Can Terrorists Build Nuclear Weapons?" in Paul Leventhal and Jonah Alexander, eds., *Preventing Nuclear Terrorism: Report and Papers of the International Task Force on Prevention of Nuclear Terrorism* (Lanham, MD: Rowan & Littlefield, 1987); and Committee on Science and Technology for Countering Terrorism, National Research Council, *Making the Nation Safer: The Role of Science and Technology in Countering Terrorism* (Washington, DC: National Academies Press, 2002), p. 45.

GAPS IN THE INTERNATIONAL RESPONSE

Success in preventing nuclear terrorism requires numerous actions across a wide array of fronts.[13] A multilayered defense strategy provides a comprehensive and balanced approach to stopping nuclear terrorism. Such a strategy involves disrupting and destroying terrorist cells, blocking terrorists from the sources of nuclear weapons and weapons-usable materials, developing and deploying radiation detection equipment, and improving intelligence assessments of when and where terrorists will launch a nuclear attack. Once terrorists acquire nuclear arms, however, stopping detonation of these weapons is exceedingly difficult. The radiation emitted by a nuclear weapon is hard to detect and easy to shield. In addition, pinpointing the time and location of a terrorist attack stretches the limits of intelligence assessments. Identifying and eradicating terrorist cells is also extremely challenging.

Although reducing the growth of terrorist groups is vitally important for the United States to have success in the wider "war on terrorism," no matter how many terrorists there are, they cannot launch a nuclear attack without access to weapons-usable nuclear materials or intact nuclear weapons. Consequently, securing and eliminating vulnerable nuclear materials and weapons offer points of greatest leverage in preventing nuclear terrorism. For these activities, much more national and international action is urgently needed to address the problems of Pakistan's highly enriched uranium and nuclear arsenal; Russia's highly enriched uranium; highly enriched uranium at more than

---

[13] For several recommendations on the various aspects of countering nuclear terrorism, see, for example, chapter two in Committee on Science and Technology for Countering Terrorism, National Research Council, *Making the Nation Safer: The Role of Science and Technology in Countering Terrorism* (Washington, DC: National Academies Press, 2002); Matthew Bunn, Anthony Wier, and John P. Holdren, *Controlling Nuclear Warheads and Materials: A Report Card and Action Plan* (Washington, DC: Nuclear Threat Initiative and the Project on Managing the Atom, Harvard University, March 2003); *The 9/11 Commission Report: Final Report of the National Commission on Terrorist Attacks Upon the United States* (New York: W.W. Norton & Company, Authorized Edition, 2004); Graham Allison, *Nuclear Terrorism: The Ultimate Preventable Catastrophe* (New York: Times Books, 2004); George Perkovich, Jessica T. Mathews, Joseph Cirincione, Rose Gottemoeller, and Jon B. Wolfsthal, *Universal Compliance: A Strategy for Nuclear Security* (Washington, DC: Carnegie Endowment for International Peace, 2005); Matthew Bunn and Anthony Wier, *Securing the Bomb 2005: The New Global Imperatives* (Washington, DC: Nuclear Threat Initiative and the Project on Managing the Atom, Harvard University, May 2005); and Charles D. Ferguson and William C. Potter with Amy Sands, Leonard S. Spector, and Fred L. Wehling, *The Four Faces of Nuclear Terrorism* (New York: Routledge, 2005).

one hundred civilian facilities in dozens of countries; and tactical nuclear weapons. Here, the focus is on how to block terrorists from acquiring these vulnerable nuclear materials and weapons.

Preventing nuclear terrorism is also closely connected to stopping the spread of nuclear weapons to other countries. By reducing the number of countries with nuclear weapons or weapons-usable nuclear materials, terrorists will have fewer places to buy or steal these critical components of nuclear terrorism. The International Atomic Energy Agency (IAEA) is at the forefront of multilateral efforts to inspect nuclear facilities to try to detect diversion of weapons-usable nuclear materials. Presently, 650 IAEA inspectors are responsible for inspecting nine hundred nuclear facilities in ninety-one countries. The annual budget of the IAEA is about $120 million—comparable to the payroll of the Washington Redskins football team.

In March 2002, the IAEA started to develop an action plan to protect against nuclear terrorism by strengthening global work to secure nuclear materials and facilities. Major parts of the plan involve leveraging the IAEA's ability to evaluate the physical security of facilities and to provide training to security personnel through services such as the International Nuclear Security Advisory Service and the International Physical Protection Advisory Service. Notably, IAEA member states must specifically request assistance from the IAEA to avail themselves of these services. Last September, the IAEA estimated that it would need at least $15.5 million annually to pay for nuclear security assistance activities for the 2006 to 2009 period. In the proposed budget, the IAEA clearly warned that its ability to carry out this plan depends on member states making sufficient contributions to the security fund. Presently, the IAEA relies on voluntary contributions to fund these activities, and contributors often impose restrictions on how their money should be spent. The IAEA has asked for "minimizing the number of conditions placed on the voluntary contributions."[14]

---

[14] International Atomic Energy Agency, *Nuclear Security—Measures to Protect Against Nuclear Terrorism*, report by the Director General, GC(49)/17, September 23, 2005.

The United States faces constraints in what security assistance it can offer Pakistan. As a signatory to the nuclear Nonproliferation Treaty (NPT), the United States is prohibited in helping a non-nuclear-weapon-state acquire nuclear explosives. Although Pakistan clearly has nuclear weapons, it is considered a non-nuclear-weapon-state under the terms of the NPT. U.S. government officials also feel constrained in how hard they can push Pakistan to improve its nuclear security and take steps to cap and eventually reduce its nuclear arsenal. Pakistan has a great deal of pride about its nuclear arsenal and relies on its nuclear weapons to offset India's conventional military superiority.

As a newly designated major non-NATO ally, Pakistan is instrumental in the Bush administration's "war on terrorism." Although President Musharraf has generally supported the fight against terrorists, he has not hunted down terrorists as much as the United States would like because he does not want to provoke the wrath of extremists seeking to topple his government. He has also refused American access to A. Q. Khan, citing Pakistan's sovereign right to handle its own affairs.

President Musharraf has repeatedly stated that Pakistan's nuclear weapons are secure. Two days after 9/11, he ordered nuclear weapon components relocated. Later that year, he also worked to root out some extremist elements in the ISI, armed forces, and nuclear weapons programs by firing his intelligence chief and some other officers, detaining suspected retired nuclear weapon scientists, and dispersing the nuclear arsenal to at least six new secret locations. President Musharraf insists that he does not want foreigners to set foot in Pakistan's nuclear installations.

Despite these security enhancements, the biggest impediment to reducing the threat of nuclear terrorism involving Pakistan is President Musharraf's expressed belief that terrorists cannot make nuclear weapons and that "the West is overly concerned" about this threat.[15] Musharraf's assumption is that terrorists would have to enrich their own uranium; in his public comments at least, he has ignored the possibility that terrorists could steal HEU weapon parts that Pakistan has already made and possesses. President Musharraf also seems to not recognize that a weapon with little military value could

---

[15] David Brunnstrom, "Dirty Bomb a Fear, Not Nuclear Terrorism, Musharraf," Reuters, April 14, 2005.

nonetheless be invaluable to terrorists. A terrorist-constructed nuclear bomb would be "the size of that sofa," he told one interviewer, pointing to a couch about six feet long. He asked, "How do you carry that?"[16] However, a six-foot-long improvised nuclear device could easily fit inside a forty-foot-long standard shipping container, probably the delivery vehicle of choice for many nuclear terrorists.

U.S. Security Assistance to Pakistan

Although it has not been reported whether the U.S. government has briefed President Musharraf about the likelihood of terrorists making a crude nuclear weapon, the United States has quietly provided some unclassified nuclear security assistance to Pakistan through what is called the U.S. Liaison Committee. Few of the details of the program have been made public.[17] Based on what is known, the United States may have helped Pakistan establish a personnel reliability program to ensure that security guards are trustworthy as well as supplied the nation with unclassified information about physical security practices and information about PAL-type security codes for nuclear warheads.

The last type of assistance is highly controversial. Some Pakistanis have expressed concern that the United States might take over control of the codes to prevent Pakistan from using its nuclear weapons. However, even if the Pakistani government has accepted this assistance, it would very likely demand absolute control over the codes. Still, President Musharraf's opponents can use this concern against him to try to characterize him as a puppet of the United States. Providing PAL codes can also run afoul of the NPT's provision not to assist another state in acquiring nuclear explosives. Although a PAL can help prevent unauthorized use of a nuclear weapon, it could promote brinkmanship because Pakistan might feel more confident in deploying PAL-protected nuclear warheads in a crisis with India.

Pakistan's warheads are widely believed to be demated—that is, the HEU is removed from the rest of the weapon. Security analysts generally applaud this posture as safer than having the weapons already assembled for firing, and some analysts argue that

---

[16] Ibid.

[17] Andrea Mitchell, "U.S. Program to Protect Pakistan's Arsenal: Covert Operations Spend Millions to Safeguard Nuclear Weapons," NBC News, February 6, 2004; and Carol Giacomo, "U.S. Helps Pakistan Safeguard Nuclear Material," Reuters, February 6, 2004.

nuclear security assistance to Pakistan should be made contingent on keeping the warheads demated.[18] Demated warheads, however, may pose a greater threat than mated warheads. Short of terrorists enlisting insider assistance to teach them how to detonate a fully assembled nuclear weapon, they would have more confidence in exploding bombs they built themselves. Another advantage for the terrorists is that presently almost all of Pakistan's nuclear weapons are powered by HEU. By stealing the HEU separated from a demated warhead, terrorists would have the material they would need to build the simplest, improvised nuclear device.

Little has been reported about what the United States is prepared to do if extremists take control of Pakistan. During her confirmation hearing in January 2005, Secretary of State Condoleezza Rice said, "We have noted this problem and we are prepared to deal with it. I would prefer not in open session to talk about this particular issue."[19] What is known is that the United States has helped with President Musharraf's personal security. Reportedly, electronic devices that the United States had provided delayed the detonation of the bomb meant to assassinate President Musharraf on December 14, 2003.[20]

In July 2002, the United States Agency for International Development (USAID) reestablished its mission to Pakistan. This USAID program concentrates on four areas: education, health, governance, and economic growth. During the first three years of this program, USAID provided about $300 million to Pakistan in these four development areas. In December 2005, the Bush administration announced that "over the next five years" it will provide Pakistan with "more than $3 billion in security, economic, and development assistance to enhance counterterrorism capacity and promote continued reform, including of the education system."[21]

---

[18] David Albright, "Securing Pakistan's Nuclear Weapons Complex," paper commissioned and sponsored by the Stanley Foundation for the forty-second Strategy for Peace Conference, Strategies for Regional Security, South Asia Working Group, October 25–27, 2001, Warrenton, Virginia.

[19] Anwar Iqbal, "U.S. Contingency Plan for Pakistani Nukes," United Press International, January 15, 2005.

[20] Dana Priest, "U.S. Aids Security of Musharraf," *Washington Post*, January 3, 2004.

[21] The White House, *Fact Sheet: Progress on the 9/11 Commission Recommendations*, December 5, 2005, available at http://www.whitehouse.gov/news/releases/2005/12/20051205-5.html, accessed on January 3, 2006.

The United States has provided security assistance for weapons-usable nuclear materials in Russia and other parts of the former Soviet Union through the Material Protection, Control, and Accounting (MPC&A) Program at a cost of nearly $1.8 billion between fiscal years 1993 and 2005. Most of this effort has involved securing Russian nuclear materials. By the end of fiscal year 2005, the U.S. National Nuclear Security Administration (NNSA) helped provide security upgrades to 80 percent of the Russian sites containing weapons-usable nuclear materials. According to the NNSA, about half (49 percent) of the materials within these sites have been secured.[22] The remaining 20 percent of the sites to be secured contain the other half of the materials.

NNSA has estimated that the Russian sites hold a total of about six hundred metric tons of nuclear materials, enough for more than forty thousand nuclear weapons. This material is outside of intact weapons, and most of it consists of HEU. Notably, this estimate is only a best guess. The United States has not done a detailed inventory of the material. Even the Russian government does not know exactly how much weapons-usable nuclear material it has. During the Cold War, when virtually all of this material was produced, the emphasis was on meeting or exceeding production quotas for producing tens of thousands of weapons and not on keeping careful track of every kilogram of material. The best unofficial estimate of the total amount of Russian military HEU, 1,020 to 1,320 metric tons, underscores the significant uncertainty in how much material actually exists.[23] An unknown, but significant, amount of this HEU remains inside Russian warheads. Continued dismantlement of these warheads will free up more HEU that will need to be secured.

NNSA officials have expressed confidence that they can complete security upgrades on the remaining sites and materials by 2008. However, Russia has not provided the United States with access to the weapons assembly and disassembly sites,

---

[22] National Nuclear Security Administration, *NNSA Expands Nuclear Security Cooperation with Russia*, fact sheet, October 2005.
[23] David Albright and Kimberly Kramer, "Fissile Material: Stockpiles Still Growing," *Bulletin of the Atomic Scientists*, November/December 2004, pp. 14–16.

which contain massive quantities of nuclear materials, especially HEU. Some Russian officials have said that they will never allow Americans into these sites.[24]

U.S.-Russian Efforts to Remove Roadblocks Barring Increased Cooperation

Within the past year, the United States and Russia have pledged to strengthen joint efforts to improve nuclear security. At the February 2005 presidential summit in Bratislava, Slovakia, U.S. President George W. Bush and Russian President Vladimir Putin agreed that their countries "bear a special responsibly for the security of nuclear weapons and fissile material, in order to ensure that there is no possibility such weapons or materials fall into terrorist hands." Specifically, they agreed to "share 'best practices' for the sake of improving security at nuclear facilities and will jointly initiate security 'best practices' consultations with other countries that have advanced nuclear programs," as well as "continue our cooperation on security upgrades and develop a plan of work through and beyond 2008 on joint projects."[25] To ensure that this plan is carried out, the presidents established a bilateral Senior Interagency Group chaired by the U.S. Secretary of Energy and the Rosatom Director. (Rosatom is the Russian Federal Atomic Energy Agency and is the successor to the Russian Ministry of Atomic Energy.)

In addition to trying to resolve the issue of obtaining access to the remaining Russian sites requiring security upgrades, this group can tackle the legal issue of extending the Nunn-Lugar Cooperative Threat Reduction (CTR) agreement, which is set to expire in June 2006. The CTR agreement provides the necessary legal protections for work to secure Russian nuclear materials as well as efforts to dismantle Russian decommissioned ballistic missiles submarines, land-based missile systems, and chemical weapons. The United States has wanted ironclad legal protections in which it will be "held harmless" in the event of an accident. Russia has requested a less rigorous liability agreement arguing that if a U.S. contractor causes an accident, Russia should not be held liable. In the summer of 2005, the United States and Russia reportedly resolved the

---

[24] Carla Anne Robbins and Alan Cullison, "Closed Doors: In Russia, Securing Its Nuclear Arsenal is an Uphill Battle Despite U.S. Help, Program Faces Resistance, Delays; Amid Chill in Relations a Warehouse Sits Empty," *Wall Street Journal*, September 26, 2005, p. A1.

[25] Office of the Press Secretary, White House, *Joint Statement by President Bush and President Putin on Nuclear Security Cooperation*, February 24, 2005, available at http://www.whitehouse.gov/news/releases/2005/02/20050224-8.html.

longstanding liability disputes in the Plutonium Disposition Agreement, which is designed to dispose of sixty-eight metric tons of weapons-grade plutonium in Russia and the United States. However, to date, the two sides have not completed this agreement. On the American side, there remains a concern that relaxing rigorous legal protections could establish a precedent in negotiations over the extension of the CTR agreement. Without a renewal, the CTR program activities would grind to a halt in Russia.

The United States wants to phase out its assistance under CTR and related programs. Russia will eventually have to take sole responsibility for operating and maintaining the security of its nuclear weapons and weapons-usable materials. Money is not the issue; Russia has earned more than enough from oil sales to fund security enhancements. Still, it has yet to spend much of its own money on nuclear security. Arguably, Russia will devote adequate resources once it makes preventing nuclear terrorism a top priority.

In addition to working with Russia on improving security at existing sites, the United States has spent about $400 million to build a highly secure storage facility to lock up Russian plutonium and highly enriched uranium. The Mayak Fissile Material Storage Facility in Siberia can hold up to one hundred metric tons of plutonium or two hundred metric tons of highly enriched uranium. Unfortunately, this facility remains empty due to delays in training security personnel and disagreements on how the United States will monitor the nuclear materials going into the storage center. The United States and Russia have reportedly agreed in principle about how to ensure that the material stored in the facility is weapons-grade, while keeping the precise composition secret, but the two sides have not reached final agreement. Also, the United States has insisted that Russia can only remove the stored material to transport it for destruction and not fabrication into new nuclear warheads. However, under this condition, Russian officials are only willing to store twenty-five metric tons of plutonium rather than fill the facility to capacity with two hundred metric tons of HEU.

On local and national levels, many Russians oppose using this facility. The Mayak region has experienced some of the worst radioactive contamination in the world, and many residents fear that if an accident occurred at the storage facility, the region would once again suffer severe environmental damage. Some Russian nationalists have condemned the storage plan as a way to trick Russia into putting its weapons-materials in a location that the United States can easily target.

Eliminating Russian Highly Enriched Uranium

Securing Russian weapons-usable nuclear materials is vitally important but not adequate. Even when these materials are in secure facilities, they are potentially vulnerable to insider theft. U.S. Department of Energy officials have acknowledged that they are most concerned about insiders at nuclear facilities collaborating with terrorists or criminals. The ultimate protection against this threat is to eliminate weapons-usable materials.

The United States has worked closely with Russia to eliminate weapons-usable fissile materials, specifically, highly enriched uranium. Starting in 1995, under the Megatons-to-Megawatts Program, Russia began converting five hundred metric tons of weapons-grade HEU (which potentially could have released "megatons" of explosive energy in a nuclear war) to non-weapons-usable low enriched form for use as nuclear reactor fuel (which produces "megawatts" of electrical power) in the United States. The conversion process is known as "down-blending" because it blends in much lower enriched forms of uranium with HEU to produce a low-enriched product. In September 2005, the conversion reached its halfway point with 250 metric tons of HEU down-blended to low-enriched fuel. Although this milestone is encouraging, it means that another ten years are required to complete the conversion of the remaining 250 tons, barring no acceleration of the program. Moreover, an estimated several hundred additional tons of Russian HEU can also be slated for elimination through this method.

Although in May 2002 Presidents Bush and Putin established an intergovernmental group to identify initiatives building on the Megatons-to-Megawatts Program, the United States and Russia have yet to agree on a new deal that would significantly expand the existing program. In 2003, however, the United States interested Russia in increasing the down-blending from 30 to 31.5 tons annually. The United States would place the resulting LEU material in a strategic fuel reserve. But the U.S. Congress declined to fund this initiative.

A major concern about a substantial expansion of the HEU conversion is that a flood of low-enriched reactor fuel could disrupt the market. If industry cannot buy in to an acceleration of the existing deal or a follow-on deal, an expansion of the program will likely never take off. Some U.S. nuclear industry officials have also expressed interest in creating a market-based incentive to promote the growth of nuclear power plants within the United States and to accelerate the consumption of weapons-grade HEU. In particular, officials at the United States Enrichment Corporation have proposed the Isaiah Project, which would set aside a reserve of fuel made from HEU to power yet-to-be-built nuclear power plants.[26]

Recently, the Nuclear Threat Initiative (NTI) released the results of a study that examined twelve options for accelerating the annual Russian HEU blend-down rate from thirty metric tons to sixty metric tons.[27] Russia presently has the capacity to convert 31.6 metric tons of weapons-grade uranium to reactor fuel.[28] Examining how much it would cost to upgrade the currently available uranium processing infrastructure in Russia, the NTI report concluded, "Accelerating HEU processing by twenty or thirty metric tons of uranium (MTU) per year requires a large amount of investment—from $1 to $1.6 billion—and a long period to introduce additional capacities (from eight to ten years)." This conclusion is based on converting the HEU to reactor fuel.

Alternatively, some analysts have recommended blending down any additional HEU stocks to the 19.9 percent enrichment level, which is just below the HEU level and is therefore very difficult to make into nuclear weapons, but is not usable as reactor fuel without additional processing because commercial reactors are typically fueled with 3 to 5 percent enriched uranium. The NTI study found that this approach could cost about $500 million of capital investment and a lead time of three to four years.

Concerning the effect of holding down-blended material off the market, the NTI report cautioned that this "would not by itself provide required market protection because market participants will anticipate the release of material at the earliest feasible opportunity and adjust their buying patterns accordingly. Therefore, additional market protection mechanisms are needed …" such as "restricting sales … to long-term contracts

---

[26] Phil Sewell, Senior Vice President, USEC, Inc., "Another Approach to Reducing Access to Weapons-Grade Nuclear Stockpiles," paper presented to the Tenth Annual International Nuclear Materials Policy Forum, Alexandria, Virginia, December 15, 2004.

[27] Laura S. H. Holgate, "Accelerating the Blend-down of Russian Highly Enriched Uranium," paper presented at the Institute for Nuclear Materials Management Annual Meeting, July 2005.

[28] Michael Knapik, "NTI Study Presents Clearer Picture of Russian HEU Downblending," *NuclearFuel*, August 29, 2005, p. 11.

... and selling the material via consortia of major industry players." Another market protection mechanism would be for "all or part of the LEU [low enriched uranium] produced from the down-blended HEU to be purchased by the U.S. government and retained as a strategic inventory."

The United States and Russia have so far missed an opportunity to expand and fund the elimination of Russian HEU. In 2002, these countries and other members of the Group of Eight (G8) industrialized countries formed the Global Partnership Against the Spread of Weapons and Materials of Mass Destruction. The partners pledged to raise $20 billion over ten years to reduce the risk of terrorists acquiring WMD, such as nuclear weapons. Despite this laudable goal, the partnership has yet to speed up elimination of the most dangerous weapons-usable nuclear material in Russia. Members of the partnership could commit to investing further in elimination of Russian HEU. Japan, for instance, relies heavily on nuclear energy for electricity production and does not have significant indigenous uranium deposits. Through the Global Partnership or on its own, Japan could offer to purchase converted Russian HEU to build up a strategic uranium reserve.[29]

CIVILIAN HIGHLY ENRICHED URANIUM

Since 1978, the United States has been working to reduce the use of highly enriched uranium in the civilian sector, including research reactors and isotope production reactors, through the Reduced Enrichment for Research and Test Reactors (RERTR) Program. RERTR has four objectives: developing LEU fuels (which are not weapons-usable) for research reactors and LEU targets for isotope production reactors (which can produce isotopes for medical treatments), conducting operational and safety studies to determine which reactors can be converted to non-weapons-usable fuels and targets; helping develop alternative, non-weapons-usable fuels and targets; and encouraging suppliers, through financial and regulatory incentives, to market only LEU fuel and

---

[29] For a similar idea that predates the Global Partnership, see Paul Leventhal and Steven Dolley, "A Japanese Strategic Uranium Reserve: A Safe and Economic Alternative to Plutonium," *Science & Global Security*, Vol. 5, 1994, pp. 1–31.

targets. Despite the efforts of this program and a parallel Russian program, more than 130 of these reactors still use HEU. Many of those reactors are located in the former Soviet Union, the European Union, and the United States.

Of the 106 research reactors currently in the RERTR program, about one-third have been fully or partially converted to LEU use; another one-third can be converted but have not been so far; and the remaining one-third require new types of reactor fuel that are in the process of being developed or still need to be developed. However, delays in developing enough types of non-weapons-usable low-enriched fuel have slowed progress in converting research reactors from using HEU.[30] Despite working to convert Soviet- and Russian-supplied reactors to LEU, Russia has yet to convert any of its many HEU-fueled reactors and has yet to commit to converting these reactors. In contrast, the United States has progressed in converting some of its research reactors and is working to accelerate these conversions. Encouragingly, China agreed in November 2005 to add its nine Miniature Neutron Source Reactors to the conversion program.

The RERTR program has set the goals of certifying high-density alternative LEU fuels by 2010 and of converting all 106 reactors to LEU use by 2014. Program scientists and engineers are attempting accelerated testing and certification, but there is currently no guarantee of successful completion of the goals. Notably, about two dozen HEU-fueled research and isotope production reactors are not included in the RERTR program. In addition, more than two dozen critical and subcritical assemblies, which are very low-powered reactors but can use significant amounts of HEU, are also not included in the program. Many of these reactors are located in Russia.

In May 2004, the United States renewed efforts to convert HEU-fueled civilian reactors and to remove HEU stored at poorly protected civilian facilities by launching the Global Threat Reduction Initiative (GTRI). The GTRI had the goal of repatriating all Soviet- and Russian-origin fresh HEU from research reactors in more than a dozen countries to Russia by the end of 2005. In addition, the GTRI aims to repatriate all Soviet- and Russian-origin spent fuel containing HEU from these reactors to Russia by

---

[30] U.S. Government Accountability Office, *Nuclear Nonproliferation: DOE Need to Take Action to Further Reduce the Use of Weapons-Usable Uranium in Civilian Research Reactors*, GAO-04-807, July 2004. The GAO report lists 105 reactors in the program. However, at the November 2005 RERTR conference, eight Russian reactors were dropped from the program, and nine Chinese reactors were included.

2010. (Much of the spent fuel has only been lightly irradiated; thus, it is susceptible to being handled safely by terrorists or thieves, and its HEU content is still weapons-usable.)

To date, the U.S. government, the Russian government, other partner governments, and the IAEA have worked together to secure Russian-origin fresh HEU from more than a half dozen countries, but the GTRI lags behind schedule. It did not complete its goal of repatriating all Soviet- and Russian-origin fresh HEU by the announced due date. The take-back of spent HEU fuel to Russia has experienced even more serious delays. The first shipment occurred in February 2006, but additional shipments could experience substantial delays because of continuing problems in completing Russian environmental impact assessments. In general, many of the HEU repatriation efforts have involved complex interactions and controversy within the U.S. government and among the participating governments.

The United States is also falling behind in repatriating U.S.-origin HEU fuel supplied to about two dozen countries. In particular, the U.S. Department of Energy has yet to reach agreement with almost half of these countries to return this fuel to the United States.[31] The GTRI has the goal of completing this repatriation by 2014. Similarly, the United States has a program to return spent HEU fuel, and this Foreign Research Reactor Spent Nuclear Fuel (FRRSNF) Acceptance Program has also fallen behind schedule. The Department of Energy has extended this program to May 2019 to allow for more time to return this material to the United States.

So-called gap materials are not covered by this program or related programs. These materials include spent fuel from foreign reactors not in the FRRSNF Acceptance Program, some fresh U.S.-origin HEU, and HEU materials that did not originate from the United States or Russia. GTRI officials have recently stated that they are planning to present a plan at the spring meeting of the European Nuclear Society's Research Reactor Fuel Management conference as to how to include the gap materials in the GTRI.

---

[31] U.S. Government Accountability Office, *Nuclear Nonproliferation: DOE Needs to Consider Options to Accelerate the Return of Weapons-usable Uranium from Other Countries to the United States and Russia*, GAO-05-57, November 2004.

Although the United States has invested in programs to convert civilian reactors to use non-weapons-usable materials, the U.S. policy toward continued use of HEU in the civilian sector has been ambiguous. According to the NNSA, which runs the GTRI, "It has long been U.S. nonproliferation policy to minimize, and *to the extent possible*, eliminate the use of highly enriched uranium (HEU) in civil nuclear programs throughout the world."[32] In effect, the United States has walked up to but has yet to embrace the policy of entirely phasing out civilian use of HEU.

In July 2005, the current U.S. policy was partially eroded when Congress passed the Energy Policy Act of 2005. The act contains an amendment that will allow the export of U.S. HEU to isotope production reactors in Canada, Belgium, France, Germany, and the Netherlands even if the producers do not commit to convert their reactors to LEU. Although the law has a "sunset provision" that the relaxation of HEU exports will be rescinded once a reliable and commercially feasible LEU technology is available for these reactors, the previous law, the 1992 Schumer amendment, stipulated that reactor operators had to commit to conversion in order to receive HEU. At the November RERTR conference, a U.S. government official stated that there are no technical barriers to converting these reactors to LEU although producers said that they still have to overcome a few technical problems.[33] The National Academy of Sciences is planning on starting a study of this issue in early 2006.

Other governments have been more forthcoming about completely phasing out civilian use of HEU. For instance, at the 2005 Nonproliferation Treaty Review Conference, Norway called for "a moratorium on the production and use of highly enriched uranium," and the Kyrgyz Republic urged "the elimination of the use of highly enriched uranium in the civilian nuclear sector."[34]

---

[32] NA-21, Office of Defense Nuclear Nonproliferation, National Nuclear Security Administration, *Reduced Enrichment for Research and Test Reactors*, Mission Statement, available at http://www.nnsa.doe.gov/na-20/rertr.shtml, accessed on December 16, 2005. (Emphasis added.)

[33] Daniel Horner, "Main Barriers to LEU Conversion for Isotopes Not Technical, U.S. Says," *NuclearFuel*, January 2, 2006.

[34] Cristina Chuen, *Reducing the Risk of Nuclear Terrorism: Decreasing the Availability of HEU*, CNS Research Story, Center for Nonproliferation Studies, May 6, 2005.

In contrast, Germany has recently opposed the trend toward not fueling civilian reactors with HEU. In 2004, Germany began operating the FRM-II reactor, which is fueled with weapons-grade uranium. Although this reactor is scheduled to convert to a lower enrichment by 2010, the operator intends to use 50 percent enriched fuel, which is still weapons-usable. An independent analysis has indicated that an enrichment level of 28 to 32 percent, which is considerably less usable for weapons, would be feasible with only minor modifications to the reactor's design.[35] Similar to Germany, Russia continues to move forward with new uses of civilian HEU-fueled reactors. In particular, Russia has added to its fleet of nuclear-powered icebreakers, and it has plans to build floating nuclear power plants, which it is trying to market to Brazil, China, India, and Indonesia.

TACTICAL NUCLEAR WEAPONS

Confusion surrounds the status and even the definition of tactical nuclear weapons, which are sometimes called nonstrategic nuclear weapons. This category of nuclear weapons is most clearly defined in the U.S.-Russia context in which strategic weapons that could readily strike the territories of the United States and Russia were subject to formal arms control treaties. In contrast, tactical nuclear weapons are usually short-range, covering less than five hundred kilometers (three hundred miles) and are generally lower yield compared to strategic nuclear weapons.

From the perspective of nuclear terrorism, tactical nuclear weapons possess some worrying characteristics. These weapons are typically intended for battlefield use and, thus, can be deployed in forward positions, which can be less secure than central storage. Tactical weapons are usually smaller and more portable than strategic weapons, making them more tempting targets for theft.

Although tactical nuclear weapons are not currently subject to formal arms control agreements, President George H. W. Bush took a bold step in 1991 as the Soviet Union was collapsing and ordered the deactivation of thousands of American tactical

---

[35] Alexander Glaser, *Neutronics Calculations Relevant to the Conversion of Research Reactors to Low-Enriched Fuel*, PhD Thesis, Darmstadt University of Technology, 2005.

nuclear weapons. Soviet President Mikhail Gorbachev soon followed with a similar step. In early 1992, President Bush ordered more U.S. nuclear forces deactivated, and Russian President Boris Yeltsin issued a similar order to Russian nuclear forces. These steps became known as the presidential nuclear initiatives. By issuing what are, in effect, gentlemen's agreements, the presidents were able to cut rapidly through bureaucratic red tape. However, in late 2004, thirteen years after the initiatives were ordered, the United States expressed concern that Russia has not fully lived up to its part of the bargain.[36] In particular, the concerns are that Russia has not dismantled all of the weapons declared under the initiatives and that it still deploys many tactical nuclear weapons outside of secure central storage. These concerns underscore that the largest remaining gap in the initiatives is the lack of transparency. The initiatives, as initially devised, did not provide for verification that the tactical nuclear weapons slated for destruction have been destroyed.

---

[36] Wade Boese, "U.S., Russia Debate Tactical Nuclear Arms," *Arms Control Today*, November 2004, p. 42.

RECOMMENDATIONS

AMERICAN STRATEGY TO PREVENT CATASTROPHIC NUCLEAR TERRORISM

The United States is not alone in confronting the threat of catastrophic nuclear terrorism. As the world's sole superpower, the United States can and should exert leadership by taking unilateral decisions and initiatives, which, once launched, can serve as the basis for stronger multilateral work. Washington should also intensify initiatives to use bilateral relationships to tackle high priority nuclear security concerns involving Pakistan and Russia. The recommendations here target gaps in existing security programs and are focused on securing and eliminating vulnerable nuclear weapons and weapons-usable nuclear materials.

Unilateral Initiatives

- To help dissuade transfers of nuclear weapons from "rogue" leaders to terrorist groups, the United States should clearly articulate a declaratory policy that it reserves the right to respond with the strongest measures including removal of those leaders from power. Washington should then urge other major powers to support this policy.[37] President Bush would have to spend considerable political capital to garner widespread support. His administration can build on the precedent it established in April 2004 when it won unanimous support in the UN Security Council for a resolution calling on countries to enact stronger controls to block terrorists from acquiring biological, chemical, or nuclear weapons. To provide necessary technical credibility to the declaratory policy, the United States should at least double the resources devoted to its nuclear explosive attribution program. This expenditure is affordable and well worth the added insurance protection. At the time of writing, this program reportedly receives at most a few tens of millions of dollars annually.

---

[37] For a more detailed discussion of this policy, see Richard N. Haass, *The Opportunity: America's Moment to Alter History's Course* (New York: Public Affairs, 2005), p. 91.

- The United States should announce an unambiguous policy that it supports delegitimizing the use of highly enriched uranium in the civilian sector. Washington should then encourage other governments to commit to this policy. When deciding to issue this policy, the United States would have to weigh the tradeoff between closing off future use of HEU for civilian purposes and taking an important effort to shutting down a route to nuclear terrorism. Fortunately, continued investment, as the United States is already doing, in developing alternative non-weapons-usable fuels for civilian nuclear reactors can make choosing to phase out civilian HEU easier to accept. As part of the political heavy lifting in carrying out this policy, the United States should enlist HEU suppliers to work toward prohibiting the export of HEU-fueled research and power reactors.[38] Any further exports should be contingent on the recipients pledging to convert their reactors to non-HEU use as quickly as is feasible. To make good on this policy, the U.S. Congress should reenact and strengthen previous restrictions on exporting highly enriched uranium to isotope production reactors.

Multilateral Initiatives

- The United States should urgently work with other leading IAEA member states to determine exactly how much additional funding the cash-strapped IAEA needs. Confronted with numerous nuclear facilities worldwide that are in need of security enhancements, at a minimum, a doubling of the $15.5 million that the IAEA has annually budgeted for its nuclear security fund is easily within the means of the United States and other major member states. This additional funding should have as few restrictions attached to it as possible. The member states should give the IAEA the authority it requires to expand its nuclear security assistance and inspection activities. Furthermore, the United States should urge member states in need of this assistance to request it.

---

[38] William C. Potter, "Meeting the Challenge of Nuclear Terrorism: Potential Threats in Asia and the Pacific," keynote address for the Asia-Pacific Conference on Nuclear Safeguards and Security, Ministerial Meeting, Sydney, Australia, November 8–9, 2004.

- The United States, Russia, the IAEA, and their partners within the Global Threat Reduction Initiative should expand the scope of the GTRI to include all currently operating HEU-fueled civilian reactors. The GTRI partners should determine which of the remaining HEU-fueled reactors really need to continue operating and which do not. Operators of the latter group should be offered incentives to shut those reactors down. Such incentives could include sharing resources with reactors still in operation and offering early retirement or other means of employment for personnel at facilities slated for shut down. For the remaining operating HEU-powered reactors, GTRI partners should determine the technical feasibility and financial costs of increasing the rate of reactor conversion. Moreover, the United States and Russia should speed up efforts to reach agreement with countries holding U.S.- and Russian-origin fresh and spent HEU fuel to repatriate these materials. The United States has already envisioned spending about $450 million in the coming years on the current GTRI program. Expanding GTRI to include all HEU-powered civilian reactors could increase costs by several tens of millions of dollars. Cost savings, however, could come about by using the targeted approach recommended here. That is, shutting down certain reactor facilities in the near term could cost less than converting, continuing to operate, and, in the long term, shutting down these facilities. The United States, Russia, and the IAEA should determine what funding the Global Partnership Against the Spread of Weapons and Materials of Mass Destruction could provide.

Bilateral Initiatives

U.S.-Pakistan Initiatives:

- If the United States has not already done so, it should offer to brief President Musharraf and a broad spectrum of Pakistani leaders to convince them that certain terrorist groups can build crude, but devastating, nuclear weapons if these groups have access to enough highly enriched uranium. If President Musharraf and other Pakistani leaders can begin to take this threat seriously, Islamabad is far more likely to take further steps to improve nuclear security.

- It is not publicly known what nuclear security assistance the United States has offered and provided Pakistan. If the United States has not already done so, it should offer security assistance that includes generic physical security procedures, unclassified military handbooks, portal control equipment, sophisticated vaults and access doors, and personnel reliability programs. These types of assistance should be designed to not spur nuclear testing, increase the likelihood of nuclear war in South Asia, harm relations with India or other countries, undermine the Pakistani government, or reveal the locations of nuclear weapons or weapons-usable nuclear materials. As a neutral party, the IAEA may be able to offer some generic physical protection assistance, through its International Physical Protection Advisory Service, without stirring concerns about foreign powers wanting to take control of Pakistan's nuclear weapons. To receive this service, Pakistan must request it, which Islamabad has not done. As a major non-NATO ally, the United States should quietly press Pakistan to reach out for this assistance. The physical protection assistance recommended here such as portal monitors and vaults would likely cost no more than about a few millions of dollars, whereas security handbooks, information about personnel reliability programs, and seminars on security procedures would cost considerably less.

U.S.-Russia Initiatives:

- If the United States can only accomplish one additional major initiative to reduce nuclear stockpiles during the remaining years of the Bush administration, it should reach agreement with Russia to accelerate and expand the successful Megatons-to-Megawatts Agreement. At the current rate of converting highly enriched uranium to reactor fuel, it would take ten more years to complete the original agreement. An estimated several hundred more tons of Russian weapons-grade HEU could become available for conversion. Each additional metric ton of weapons-grade HEU that is eliminated would reduce the risk of nuclear terrorism by approximately twenty crude nuclear weapons, assuming that terrorists would need about fifty kilograms of this material to make one weapon. Although there are various ways to accelerate and expand the Megatons-to-Megawatts Agreement, probably the most promising method would form a consortium of the U.S. government, Russia, major nuclear industry companies, as well as countries that have significant investments in nuclear energy use and are participating in the Global Partnership. Such a consortium would achieve buy-in from industry and would share the burden by bringing in a wide array of contributors with a vested interest in creating fuel for nuclear power plants. The more contributors to the consortium, the fewer capital costs would be needed from each contributor. Expanding the existing program would require upwards of a few billion dollars of capital costs and a construction time of eight to ten years. The nuclear fuel created could be set aside in strategic reserves for existing nuclear reactors or dedicated to fueling new nuclear plants or some combination of these two plans.

- Washington and Moscow should quickly resolve access issues to complete security upgrades at the remaining 20 percent of Russian facilities containing about half of Russia's stockpile of weapons-usable nuclear materials by 2008 or earlier. Such security upgrades would not increase costs beyond what the United States is already budgeting to spend under the Material Protection, Control, and Accountancy Program. Both President Bush and President Putin should demand frequent updates of the intergovernmental working group that is trying to solve this access problem, and they should be prepared to step in to expedite achieving access to the remaining sites. The United States has provided Russia reciprocal access to a sensitive U.S. nuclear site. More of this type of reciprocity may be needed to gain greater cooperation between the United States and Russia. In addition, an inventory of Russian weapons-usable nuclear material is needed to determine how much security work remains to be done. Furthermore, the United States and Russia should rapidly resolve disputes over the empty Mayak Fissile Material Storage Facility. As the United States has already paid about $400 million for this facility, it should be willing to pay the additional political cost to expedite filling it with weapons-usable nuclear material, giving priority to HEU.

- The United States and Russia should work together to secure and reduce tactical nuclear weapons that are more portable and forward deployed than strategic nuclear arms and thus can be more susceptible to terrorist acquisition. To achieve Russian agreement for substantial dismantlement of its tactical nuclear weapons, the United States should be prepared to remove and dismantle American tactical nuclear weapons based in Europe. In a related recommendation, the United States and Russia should formalize an agreement to verify the status of the tactical nuclear weapons slated for dismantlement under the presidential nuclear initiatives. Completion of these recommendations could cost tens to hundreds of millions of dollars depending on the number of weapons to be secured or eliminated. The United States and Russia should approach the Global Partnership for financial support.

Although full implementation of these recommendations will still leave a residual risk of devastating nuclear terrorism because of the continuing existence of nuclear arsenals and the enduring peril of nuclear proliferation, rapid national and international action will substantially reduce the risk that terrorists can seize or make nuclear weapons.

ABOUT THE AUTHOR

Charles D. Ferguson is a fellow for science and technology at the Council on Foreign Relations. He is also an adjunct assistant professor in the School of Foreign Service at Georgetown University and an adjunct lecturer at the Johns Hopkins University. Before coming to the Council, he was scientist-in-residence at the Center for Nonproliferation Studies of the Monterey Institute of International Studies. At the Center, he codirected a project that systemically assessed how to prevent and respond to nuclear and radiological terrorism. This project's major findings were published in *The Four Faces of Nuclear Terrorism* (Routledge, 2005). He is also the lead author of the award-winning report *Commercial Radioactive Sources: Surveying the Security Risks*, which examined the threat of radiological dispersal devices, such as "dirty bombs."

In addition, Dr. Ferguson has worked on nuclear safety issues in the Nonproliferation Bureau at the U.S. Department of State and analyzed nonproliferation and arms control issues at the Federation of American Scientists. He has done scientific research at the Los Alamos National Laboratory, the Space Telescope Science Institute, the Harvard-Smithsonian Center for Astrophysics, and the University of Maryland. After graduating with distinction from the U.S. Naval Academy, he served as a nuclear engineering officer on a ballistic-missile submarine. He holds a PhD in physics from Boston University.

OTHER COUNCIL SPECIAL REPORTS
SPONSORED BY THE COUNCIL ON FOREIGN RELATIONS

Getting Serious About the Twin Deficits
Menzie D. Chinn
CSR No. 10, September 2005

Both Sides of the Aisle: A Call for Bipartisan Foreign Policy
Nancy E. Roman
CSR No. 9, September 2005

Forgotten Intervention? What the United States Needs to Do in the Western Balkans
Amelia Branczik and William L. Nash
CSR No. 8, June 2005

A New Beginning: Strategies for a More Fruitful Dialogue with the Muslim World
Craig Charney and Nicole Yakatan
CSR No. 7, May 2005

Power-Sharing in Iraq
David L. Phillips
CSR No. 6, April 2005

Giving Meaning to "Never Again": Seeking an Effective Response to the Crisis in Darfur and Beyond
Cheryl O. Igiri and Princeton N. Lyman
CSR No. 5, September 2004

Freedom, Prosperity, and Security: The G8 Partnership with Africa: Sea Island 2004 and Beyond
J. Brian Atwood, Robert S. Browne, and Princeton N. Lyman
CSR No. 4, May 2004

Addressing the HIV/AIDS Pandemic: A U.S. Global AIDS Strategy for the Long Term
Daniel M. Fox and Princeton N. Lyman
Cosponsored with the Milbank Memorial Fund
CSR No. 3, May 2004

Challenges for a Post-Election Philippines
Catharin E. Dalpino
CSR No. 2, May 2004

Stability, Security, and Sovereignty in the Republic of Georgia
David L. Phillips
CSR No. 1, January 2004

To order hard copies, please call: 800-537-5487.
Note: All these reports are available on the Council's website at www.cfr.org., along with a complete list of the Council publications since 1998. For more information, contact publications@cfr.org.